Take Zawn with you!

by Peter Millett
illustrated by Russ Daff

CAMBRIDGE
UNIVERSITY PRESS

UCL
Institute of Education

Rehan and Aahil ran to the beach.

'Let's go surfing,' Aahil shouted.

'Cool,' Rehan said.

'Wait,' said Mum. 'You have to take Zayan with you.'

3

Zayan went with Rehan and Aahil.

They went into the sea.

He looked scared. 'The waves are too big for me!'

He went back to the beach.

Rehan looked at Aahil.

'No more surfing for us today,' he said.

Later, Rehan and Aahil wanted to go skateboarding.

They had to take Zayan, too.

Zayan went on the skateboard.

6

'I can't do this,' he said. 'It's too hard.'

'No more skateboarding for us today,' said Rehan.

'We need to find something that Zayan can do too,' Aahil said.

Then they looked at Zayan.

'What are you doing?' Aahil said to Zayan.

'I want to try sandboarding,' he said.

Aahil looked at Rehan and smiled.

'Okay, let's go sandboarding,' he said.

'Cool,' Zayan said.

So Aahil, Rehan and Zayan went down
to the sand dunes.

Sandboarding was fun.

They went down the sand dunes again and again.

'Look at me!' said Zayan. 'I am the fastest.'

Soon it was time to go home.

'No more sandboarding for us today,' Rehan said.

Zayan didn't want to go.

'Can I come back tomorrow?' he said.

'Yes,' Mum said.

'But you have to take Rehan and Aahil with you, too.'

Take Zayan with You! ✏️ Peter Millett

Teaching notes written by Sue Bodman and Glen Franklin

Using this book

Developing reading comprehension

Three young brothers go to the seaside with their parents. His big brothers have to look after Zayan. This will reflect the experiences of children who are older and younger siblings. Zayan can't surf or skateboard, but he discovers he can sand-board. The twist in the story is that this is something his bigger brothers can't do!

Grammar and sentence structure

- Contractions ('*Can't*', '*Let's*') reflect natural speech patterns.
- Varied, longer sentences with adverbial words and phrases ('*today*', '*again and again*').

Word meaning and spelling

- Multisyllabic words ('*skateboarding*') require children to identify parts on words.
- Topic-specific words ('*sand dunes*', '*surfing*').

Curriculum links

Science – The story could provide the start for work on forces and momentum

Social Science – Looking after siblings, and caring for each other. Also, that different people have different strengths and skills that we value.

Learning outcomes

Children can:

- track accurately across multiple lines of print without pointing
- solve new words by identifying known chunks with words, whilst attending to context and grammar
- discuss character motive and explain reasons for actions.

A guided reading lesson

Book Introduction

Activate children's prior experiences of beaches and of beach activities. (For children living in regions without access to the sea, you could share non-fiction texts or on-line video footage of surfers and skateboarders.)

Give each child a copy of the book. Read the title and the blurb with them.

Orientation

Ask who has a younger brother or sister, and talk about when and how they might have to look after them.

Give a brief overview of the book:

In this book, Zayan goes to the beach with his family. His big brothers want to do some fun things at the beach, but they have to take Zayan with them. Shall we find out what happens?

Preparation

page 2: Point out that the boys are going surfing. Find the word and read it, isolating the two separate parts '*surf-ing*'. Check children know what this means, using the picture to help.

Say: *Mum tells Rehan and Aahil 'you have to take Zayan with you'. Can you find that line on the page? Let's read it like Mum would say it. Why does she say that, do you think?* Elicit that they are the big brothers and have to look after their younger brother; they need to keep him safe on the beach.

Page 5: Ask: *Why do Rehan and Aahil say 'No more surfing for us today'. Yes, because Zayan can't surf, can he? So they have to find something else to do.*

Turn to the next page and say: *Now they are going to try skateboarding. Do you think Zayan will be able to do this? It looks hard for a little boy. How do you think he's feeling?*